Fifty Funny Teacher Moments

Hilary Coussens

Illustrations by

Ruth Hope

TO THE MEMORY OF
RICHARD MAYNE

Richard was a delightful and fun-loving student whom I had the privilege of teaching before he moved on to Leeds University to study Mathematics and Finance. He was an inspiration to others, both by the conscientious way he approached his studies and by the humour he injected into every lesson. Richard devastatingly lost his life when Malaysia Airlines flight MH17 was shot down over Ukraine in July 2014. He had so much potential, and is enormously missed by his family and friends.

CONTENTS

ACKNOWLEDGEMENTS

I wish to thank all students whom I have had the pleasure of teaching during my career, especially those who instigated the various occurrences related in this book. Names have been changed unless a student has consented to their name being present. Thanks are also due to colleagues who provided examples to redress the balance away from predominantly Mathematics and Religious Studies incidents.

Mention is also due to a special granddaughter who had the idea of collecting these anecdotes into the form of a small book.

NEEDS OF A HORSE

Children love to spot cows and sheep when taken on a coach outing. On one occasion Harriet spotted a horse in a field. In the middle of the field was a solitary mobile toilet.

'Why is there a toilet in the field?' she asked.

'Perhaps it is for the horse,' joked her teacher.

'But the horse is too big for the toilet,' Harriet said.

Her teacher simply replied that the horse would have to reverse into the toilet.

PERCENTAGES FOR BREAKFAST

A new pupil arrived into Year 10 and was assigned to the 'bottom set' for Mathematics. The first topic to be studied in September concerned percentages.

'Where in life have you come across percentages,' his teacher asked the class.

'Every day I use percentages at breakfast, because I have 50% Cornflakes and 50% Weetabix,' was Richard's contribution.

A few weeks later he was proud to announce that these percentages had been adjusted due to the introduction of Coco-pops.

This delightful student later studied Mathematics at 'A' level and at University. One never can tell the outcome of percentages!

DECENCY REQUIRED IN CLASS

Oliver was a hard-working student in Year 11. He did, however, have an annoying habit of rolling up a trouser leg as far as his knee and placing the corresponding foot on his chair, thereby revealing one hairy leg.
Without thinking to gather the most appropriate words, his teacher exclaimed, 'Put your trousers down, Oliver!'.

WATCH OUT FOR TRAFFIC LIGHTS

Can teachers be excused for being tired at the end of a day?

When music teacher Mr. Williams was driving home from school he was convinced that he had seen green traffic lights. Unfortunately the green lights were intended for traffic coming from another direction. Mr. Williams had just driven over red lights. A police car drew up alongside him, and Mr. Williams made his confession.

The police officer responded that he could completely understand what had happened, because he had been a pupil of Mr. Williams at school.

Mr. Williams was forgiven, but went on to be a music teacher in a prison.

UNPLEASANT SUMS

Five-year-old Parisha arrived home from school.

Her mother asked, 'What did you do in school today?'

Parisha replied that she had enjoyed her Mathematics lesson. She said that she had been learning about 'odd numbers and evil numbers.'

PILOT VERSUS PILATE

 A Year 7 class had been considering the narrative concerning the trial of Jesus, and wished to act out the trial by improvisation. As the pupils were doing this, their teacher took up her observation post at the back of the classroom. She seldom interrupted, but at one point felt it was necessary to enquire: 'Who is that standing next to Pilate?'

 'That is the co-pilot,' came Sam's reply.

THE SCHOOL PHOTOGRAPHER'S REAL ROLE

The Head teacher of a secondary school tried hard to relate well with his pupils and to get to know them, rather than becoming inundated with paper work. To help him in this task, he took photographs of new pupils as they arrived in Year 7, with the permission of their parents.

At the end of term he incorporated some of these photographs into his assembly talk. Little did he know that Luke would go home and say to his father: 'The photographer took our assembly this morning.'

LEAD US NOT INTO TEMPTATION

Many years ago Mr. Brown willingly gave up his half term holiday to take a Duke of Edinburgh expedition from Leicestershire to Derbyshire, where his pupils were to camp near to Trent Lock.

When the party arrived at Trent Station, Vikram was disappointed to notice that the 'facilities' were rather rudimentary. He declared to Mr. Brown that his disappointment was to be expected. After all, each morning in school assembly, he had been saying: 'Lead us not into Trent Station'

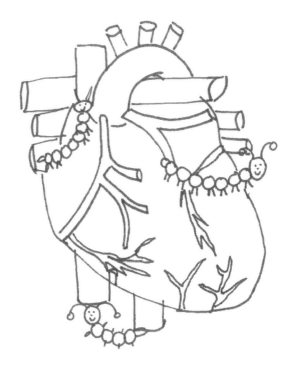

CRAWLING BLOOD VESSELS

 Alex was assigned a Biology home-work which involved describing the various types of blood vessels in the human body.

 He explained that arteries carry blood away from the heart, that 'vanes' carry blood back to the heart and that 'caterpillars' connect the arteries to the vanes.

FOOD FOR THOUGHT

Jenna remarked to the school dinner lady that she could not possibly eat tongue meat as she could never bring herself to eat something which came out of an animal's mouth.

The dinner lady replied by asking Jenna how she could have managed to eat the sponge pudding earlier in the week, as several eggs went in to the making of this.

RESERVOIRS MUST NOT RUN DRY

A serious water shortage one hot summer caused concern regarding the level of water in reservoirs. As a Geography teacher was discussing this with his students, he asked his class for ideas to help with this situation.

'Ask all homeowners to fill a bucket with water from their tap, take it to the nearest reservoir and pour it in,' contributed Anna.

ANTENNAE OF AN INSECT

Biology lessons, at one stage, included a study of antennae in insects and the possible reasons why they exist.

Ben's explanation was that an insect which has antennae was an insect which has ten eyes in order to see much of the surrounding area.

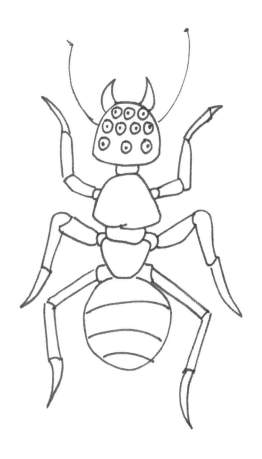

DANGEROUS LIFE OF A CLERGYMAN

Arvind was writing up his Science experiment done earlier in the day.

'To heat up the water we placed a thermometer and the water in a deacon. We then placed the deacon onto a piece of gauze. We then put the gauze on a tripod and lit the Bunsen burner under the tripod,' he wrote.

TAKING THE VICAR LITERALLY

A Remembrance Day service was being held in the local parish church. The time came for the pupils to sit down as the lesson was read.

Instead of announcing: 'Please sit down', the vicar preferred the flowery language of: 'Would the congregation please take up their seats.'

You can imagine the commotion as the pupils then tried lifting their seats from the ground.

Earlier that day, Naomi requested: 'Please Sir, would you let us listen to the radio so we can hear the two-minute silence?'

TEACHERS MUST BE CAREFUL HOW THEY SPEAK

Teachers are familiar with the fact that it is extremely difficult to engage in classroom discussions when several people try and talk at the same time.

Mr. Smith vented his impatience at the constant interruptions by class members by exclaiming: 'Every time I open my mouth some fool speaks!'

HELP WITH CHILDBIRTH

For her Biology homework, Ellie needed to comment on the birth of a baby.

She wrote: 'A woman knows when her baby is going to arrive because she starts to have contraptions.'

OLD TESTAMENT
MISCONCEPTIONS

The Old Testament may, in parts, be fascinating, but difficult, to understand.

Adam's written account concerning Solomon was that he had: 'seven hundred wives and three hundred cucumbers.'

RELATING MATHS TO REAL LIFE SITUATIONS

Miss Coles was checking that her pupils knew the mathematical names for certain types of quadrilaterals.
 She obtained the correct names for the square, rectangle, rhombus and parallelogram. But when she pointed to a trapezium, Megan responded: 'That is a pair of underpants.'

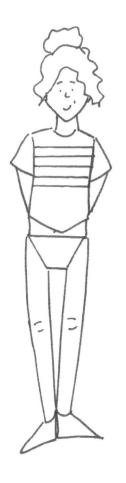

HAPPY MARRIAGE

Part of the Religious Studies syllabus involved considering a Christian perspective on marriage.

An examination candidate had been to a wedding service and heard the words: 'In sickness and in health.'

His examination response included that: 'In marriage the couple make a promise to stay together in thickness and in wealth.'

UNDERSTANDING A PROOF

A topic in the 'A' level Mathematics syllabus is entitled 'Proof.' One way of proving something is called: 'Proof by Contradiction.'

A hypothesis is proved to be true by first considering what would happen if it was not true. Then, if it is impossible to be 'not true', it must be true!

Perhaps it was this idea which was in the mind of Lizzie when she declared that: 'If someone gives a wrong answer to a right question then it must be right.'

EXERCISE BOOKS

Mathematics teacher Mr. Prescott really needed a shopping basket in order to transport his pupils' exercise books around the school. But he preferred to carry the books in his arms.

He was prone to say, when leaving a class: 'Hold the door open for me so that I can pass out.'

MUDDLED FORGIVENESS

 Harry was in a Year 6 lesson when pupils were discussing possible reasons why people go to church.

 Harry's contribution was that they may decide to go to church in order to: 'confuse their sins.'

ABSENCE FROM SCHOOL

Deputy Head-teacher Miss Sizzling had the responsibility of ensuring that all pupils who were absent from school on a particular day were accounted for.

An email arrived in her inbox which read: 'My daughter is not in school today because she is under the doctor.' Miss Sizzling replied that she hoped the pupil would soon recover.

HEALTH AND SAFETY

Chemistry lessons had rather confused Jack. When asked to write about the dangers of carbon monoxide, he wrote: 'If you smell a gas which does not have an odour, then it is bound to be carbon monoxide.'

VIOLIN TONE DESTROYED

Aniko arrived for her violin lesson feeling distraught. Her peripatetic music teacher asked why she was upset. She explained that, whilst practising at home, she put her violin on the table and left the room for a moment. In her absence the family dog had climbed onto the table and was responsible for three large claw marks on her instrument. So Aniko polished her violin with the house floor polish to try and cover up the scratches.

Little did she know that, by not using the appropriate instrument polish, the quality of tone produced by her violin had deteriorated considerably.

PERAMBULATING IN THE PARK

English teacher Mrs. Bailey was helping pupils to widen their vocabulary.

Her class was asked to incorporate different words into a sentence which made sense to them.

'I went to the park and I saw a lady pushing a pram so she was perambulating,' wrote Hannah.

DISAPPEARING TEACHER

Mr. Edwards was a Mathematics teacher who demanded full attention from his students at all times.

So the sentence he tended to use every lesson, to the amusement of his pupils, was: 'Watch the board while I run through it.'

SCHOOL-BAKED CAKES

 A Home Economics lesson consisted of Year 7 pupils working in small groups to bake cupcakes. Most pupils were delighted to view the results of their work through the oven doors. Cakes were seen to be rising beautifully, but one group expressed disappointment to the teacher.

 'There are two ovens,' she said, 'so put your cakes in the oven which you lit.'

PARTS OF THE ANATOMY

Secondary school Biology teacher Mr. Jones discovered, through his marking, that most pupils in his class were unable to spell correctly the name for a certain part of the male anatomy. They had spelt the word in a similar way to how it was pronounced.

During the following lesson he decided to get the class to chant the word repeatedly in the way in which it was spelt. Little did he know that, at this precise moment, his Head-teacher would walk through the classroom door alongside potential parents who were being shown around the school.

LUMINOUS JACKETS

One winter's day Marwa remarked that the teacher on duty by the main school gates, who was ensuring safety at the start of the school day, was wearing a 'high visibility' jacket in order to be luminous.

She entered her form room and announced: 'Mr. Taylor is lunatic today.'

SCHOOL PHOTOCOPIER

Mrs. Simpson was an English teacher who could hardly wait for the day when she retired. She was due to retire just after her sixtieth birthday.

Each teacher had a unique password in order to use the staff photocopier, but their numbers were invariably forgotten. They did, however, know Mrs. Simpson's, as it was derived from the birthday she was anticipating. Therefore other members of staff used her password, until the Head-teacher, keen to save money, announced in a staff meeting: 'There is one member of staff who uses 72% of the total photocopying budget!'

THE DANGER OF BREATHING

Nadine had been learning about respiration in her Science lessons. When recording in her exercise book what she had learnt, she wrote: 'When you breathe in you inspire and when you breath out you expire.'

FORCED TOGETHERNESS

Rahul enjoyed thinking about the meaning of words and their significance.

Discussions on marriage in PSHCE lessons resulted in him remarking that he believed the aim of getting married is to stay together for life, and that this is why the word 'wedlock' is used to describe the happy event.

IMPROVISING ON EQUIPMENT

Mathematics teachers can sometimes have a difficult time encouraging all pupils to bring the necessary equipment to lessons. This includes items such as protractors, pencils, rulers and calculators.

A more accommodating Mr. Wilson was heard to say: 'If you do not have a rubber use the boy's behind.'

MOVING HOUSE

James was a young boy who explained to his teacher that, at the week-end, his family would be 'moving house.' His teacher showed interest, and asked him if this would take place in one day.

'Only if the lorry picking up the house can make the journey in one day,' James replied.

THE WILL TO LIVE

Mrs. Coleman was approaching retirement after a long career in teaching. One Friday at break-time she announced in the staff room that she was going to see her solicitor the following day to get a free 'will check.'

Her colleague on the other side of the room could not hear clearly amongst all the chatter.

'You are going to get a free wheel chair tomorrow?' she asked in reply.

PRACTICAL DETENTIONS

Several years ago the senior management of a school decided to change what happened in school detentions. Instead of copying out the school rules or writing an apology letter for their misdemeanor, pupils were assigned several wooden desks which had unfortunately been defaced over the years.

They were told to: 'run up and down the desks with a piece of sandpaper.'

VISCOSITY OF A LIQUID

A Science teacher was starting to explain that a liquid which is more viscous is a liquid which is 'thicker', perhaps like honey.

Robert had been reading about this in his text book, and wrote that some liquids can be more 'vicious' than others. When his teacher pointed out his spelling mistake he was happy to relate that 'vicious' was a more appropriate description of his hamster, who had bitten him that morning.

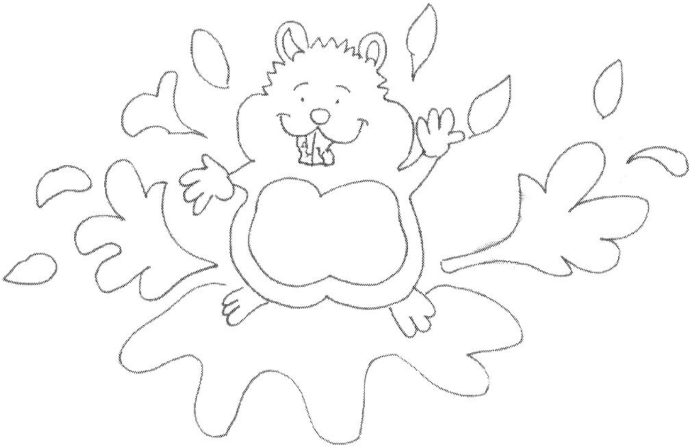

HAPPINESS TOGETHER?

In Religious Studies Charlotte had been studying differing views on marriage associated with different religions.

Instead of answering a question on her school examination paper concerning wedding promises with the words: 'Till death us do part,' she wrote: 'To death we depart.'

'APPING' ON THE COMPUTER

English teacher Mrs. Woodward could not understand what was meant by the word 'apping' in Amanda's homework.

On returning the homework she asked Amanda what she meant by the word. Amanda explained confidently that 'apping' is the word needed when we use an iPad to put an app on it.

ANGELS IN MATHEMATICS

Some examination questions in the Shape and Space part of the mathematics course require candidates to write a reason explaining each stage of their calculation.

'The angels inside a triangle add up to 180 degrees,' wrote Sophie on her examination paper.

TECHNICALITIES FOR BEING EXCUSED

'Please can I go to the toilet?' asked Joe to his English teacher. His teacher, Miss Kenworthy, was a perfectionist. She would have preferred Joe to ask: 'Please may I go to the toilet?'
 'I don't know,' said Miss Kenworthy.
 She could not resist adding: 'Can you go?'

FLOWERS IN NATURE

It was time to appreciate the wonders of nature. A primary school teacher pointed to the flowers outside the classroom window, saying to her class; 'Look at all those begonias.'

Larissa put up her hand and said: 'Yes, and I can see some little ones as well.'

GENERATING ELECTRICITY

An investigation in Physics involved written work concerning the generation of electricity.
George did well in his writing about wind turbines and solar farms, but accidentally used the words: 'plant pot' instead of 'power plant' in his conclusions.

ORNAMENTS IN MUSIC

An 'A' level music group was studying baroque music. Their work concluded with a test, in which students were asked the question: 'What is an ornament in music.'

'An ornament in music is when the musician shows off in a bar,' wrote Becky.

STAND TO ATTENTION IN ASSEMBLY

For several years a primary school pupil named Emma always came out of her school assembly with her arms tucked firmly into her sides.

It was only later that she discovered that the final words spoken were not: 'arm in,' but was 'Amen.'

HYGIENE WHEN SHOPPING

 Home Economics lessons need to stress the importance of hygiene.

 But this does not make it acceptable for a pupil to write: 'When we select the cakes we wish to buy in a shop, and they are not already wrapped, we must use the tongues provided instead of our hands.'

WEDDED BLISS

It must be sad for children when the happiness in their parents' relationship turns to arguments and unhappiness.

Marriage is a topic which is sometimes under debate. Was it a slip whereby Grace wrote: 'All people should marry someone sooner rather than later so that they can endure family life'?

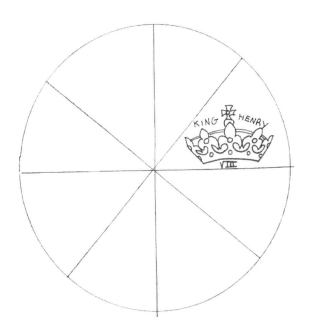

PIE CHARTS IN HISTORY

 It is sometimes thought that the concept of fractions does not always come easily to young children.

 It is no wonder, therefore, that Jacob's idea of illustrating one-eighth as a fraction of a Pie chart was to write: 'Henry VIII' inside one of the sectors of his diagram.

DISCIPLINE ESSENTIALS

Mrs. Harvey arrived at her first teaching post after qualifying as a French teacher. She was assigned to a classroom on the first floor of the school, and was intrigued to find that there was a parachute canopy in the classroom cupboard.

When asking her Head of Department why it was there, she was told that a pupil had jumped out of the window when being taught by the teacher whose post she had filled. The pupil was unharmed, but not so the self-esteem of the teacher.

So much for instilling confidence in a newly-qualified teacher!

ABOUT THE AUTHOR

Hilary Coussens (nee Edwardes), the daughter of a Leicestershire Headmaster, studied Mathematics and Statistics at Leeds and Cambridge universities and Christian Theology in Bristol. She went on to teach Mathematics and Religious Studies in a wide variety of schools in Cambridgeshire, Bristol, Surrey, Warwickshire and Leicestershire. She aimed to create an atmosphere in lessons of enjoyment and openness to contribute to the lessons, rather than holding back for fear of failing. Though this has met with varying success, she hopes adults can look back and remember their teachers for the pleasant atmosphere they inculcated in a classroom, as much as the grades acquired in examinations. She tried never to cause uneasiness when incidents such as those related in this book occurred.

 She is proud that Ruth Hope was one of her pupils, and grateful to her for providing the illustrations. Ruth is now enjoying studying Performance Costume at Edinburgh University.

061

Printed in Great Britain
by Amazon.co.uk, Ltd.,
Marston Gate.